CRITICAL
THINKING
PUZZLES

Michael A. DiSpezio

Illustrated by Myron Miller

Sterling Publishing Co., Inc. New York

Library of Congress Cataloging-in-Publication Data

Dispezio, Michael A.
    Critical thinking puzzles / by Michael A. DiSpezio; illustrated
by Myron Miller.
        p.   cm.
    Includes index.
    ISBN 0-8069-9430-4
    1. Puzzles. 2. Critical thinking. I. Miller, Myron, l948– .
II. Title.
GV1493.D55   1996
793.73—dc20   96–28211
                                                        CIP

            7 9 10 8

Published by Sterling Publishing Company, Inc.
387 Park Avenue South, New York, N.Y. 10016
© 1996 by Michael A. DiSpezio
Distributed in Canada by Sterling Publishing
c/o Canadian Manda Group, One Atlantic Avenue, Suite 105
Toronto, Ontario, Canada M6K 3E7
Distributed in Great Britain and Europe by Cassell PLC
Wellington House, 125 Strand, London WC2R 0BB, England
Distributed in Australia by Capricorn Link (Australia) Pty Ltd.
P.O. Box 6651, Baulkham Hills, Business Centre, NSW 2153,
Australia
Manufactured in the United States of America
All rights reserved

Sterling ISBN 0-8069-9430-4

CONTENTS

✦ ✦ ✦

Acknowledgments

Very few things are produced (or solved) in a vacuum. It is through the nurture, encouragement, playfulness, and caring of others that books such as *Critical Thinking Puzzles* are created.

With sincere gratitude, I recognize the support of my parents, Joseph and Anne DiSpezio, my sister, Vivian Demarco, and her bright and talented family, my editor, Hazel Chan, my wife, Susan, my friends and colleagues at NSTA, and my caffeine buddies at Coffee O.

I'd also like to thank my son, Anthony, for being an "awesome" puzzle tester.

INTRODUCTION

When we think critically we are engaging in intellectual strategies to probe the basic nature of a problem, situation, or puzzle. By these strategies, we mean making observations, predictions, generalizations, reasonings by assumptions, comparisons and contrasts, uncovering relationships between the parts to the whole, and looking for sequences. It sounds like a lot, but everyone has these skills and the puzzles in this book are designed to challenge, exercise, and stretch the way you interpret the world.

Some of the puzzles here are old favorites that have entertained people for years. Several of them are presented in their time-tested way. Most of the standards, however, have a new twist or updated story added. Other puzzles require some inventive solutions, so don't be afraid to be creative. Most of them can be done with a pencil or pen.

Some require inexpensive material that can probably be found around the house: a pair of scissors, markers, tape, toothpicks, and a yardstick. Even though some puzzles can be solved using algebra, they were selected for their ability to be visualized and figured out this way. Therefore, in addition to being fun to do, they offer an arena to practice thinking skills.

Statements such as "I want you to memorize this list!" or "That's a good answer, but it wasn't the one I expected" help to extinguish critical thought.

Although you'll never have to measure an ant's path or alter a flag, the process of creating and evaluating a reasonable answer is a worthwhile experience. By the time you finish this book, those powerful skills will be back on track, probing your everyday experiences for a more thorough and deeper understanding.

Ready to start? Great, because the fun is about to begin.

—Michael

THE PUZZLES

Pyramid Passage

✦ ✦ ✦

Ancient Egyptian pyramids were built as royal tombs. Within these massive stone structures were rooms, halls, and connecting passageways. Look at the figure below. Can you draw four paths that connect the matching symbols? The paths may not cross, they may not enter a non-matching pyramid, nor may they go outside the large pyramid boundary.

Answer on page 72.

Magic Pyramid

✦ ✦ ✦

For this pyramid, can you place the numbers 1,2,3,4,5, and 6 in the circles shown below? Only one number may be placed in a circle and all numbers must be used. When the final arrangement is complete, the sum of each side's three numbers must all be the same number.

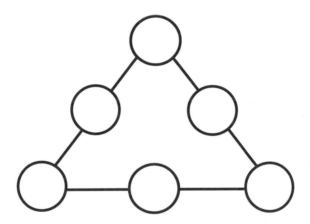

Answer on page 72.

Pyramid Builders

✦ ✦ ✦

The Egyptian pyramids at Giza are incredible structures that took many years to complete. They were constructed out of large rectangular stone blocks, each weighing about as much as a car. The two largest pyramids contain over two million of these blocks!

Now, it's your turn to work. Can you build a three dimensional pyramid using two odd-shaped blocks?

Copy the figure below onto two pieces of stiff paper. Fold along the inner lines as shown and use tape to secure the edges.

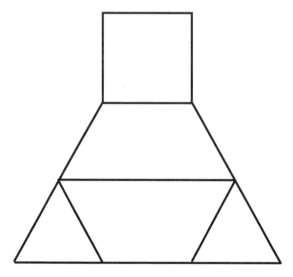

Now arrange the blocks to form a pyramid with four sides.

Answer on page 72.

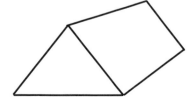

Trial by Triangle

✦ ✦ ✦

Take a look at these two identical triangles. They are made with six sticks.

Can you rearrange the sticks so that they form four triangles? All of the new triangles must be the same size as these original two!

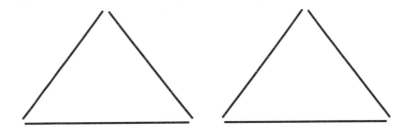

Answer on page 73.

By the way, here's a triangle that you can draw but can't build. It's called an impossible triangle. See why?

Before you go on to the next puzzle, take at look at these strange objects. Do you think that they can also be built? Or do you think there may be some sort of trick?

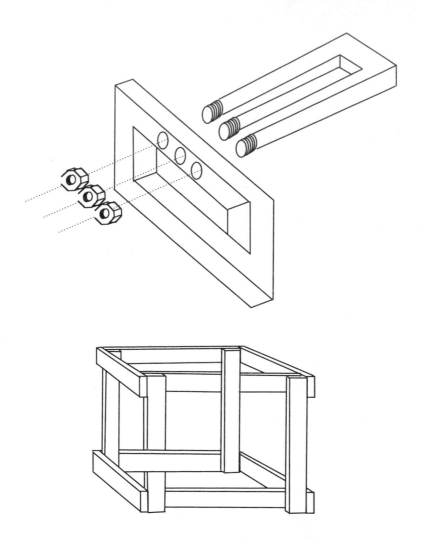

Answer on page 73.

Trapezoid 2 Triangle

✦ ✦ ✦

Here's another triangle whose only problem is that it isn't built yet. You'll have to assemble it from these three trapezoids!

Answer on page 73.

Spare My Brain

✦ ✦ ✦

To move their armies, the Romans built over 50,000 miles of roads. Imagine driving all those miles! Now imagine driving those miles in the first gasoline-driven car that has only three wheels and could reach a top speed of about 10 miles per hour.

For safety's sake, let's bring along a spare tire. As you drive the 50,000 miles, you rotate the spare with the other tires so that all four tires get the same amount of wear. Can you figure out how many miles of wear each tire accumulates?

Answer on page 73.

Whirling Paradox

Let's take a closer look at those tires. If a car with spoke wheels drives by, we will see that when the spinning spokes get to the top of the wheel, they are moving so fast that they become blurred. At the same time, the spokes on the bottom half of the wheel appear to be moving much slower. In fact, they are so slow that you may be able to count them. If the spokes are connected to the same wheel, how can this be?

HINT: There may be a connection between this observation and the sound of a speeding car as it zooms by.

Answer on page 74.

Lost?

Now we're on foot. Imagine that you and several friends have hiked into a remote region of the countryside. Your final destination is the land of Ultima. After leaving the village of Skullara, you continue following the trail and come across an important intersection. There is, however, one slight problem.

The sign showing which way to go has been knocked down. How can you figure out what is the right direction you need to go?

Answer on page 74.

Sand Traps

♦ ♦ ♦

As you continue on your hike, you're handed a map of the terrain ahead. This is not a safe place. In fact, the entire region is filled with quicksand, which is shown on the map as black splotches. Contrary to belief, quicksand does not suck or pull you under. Instead, it's your weight that makes you sink in this water and fine sand mixture.

Your challenge is to discover a path from any point on the bottom edge of the map to any point on the top edge without running into quicksand (black splotches). To make it more challenging, the path must consist of only two straight lines.

To start, place your pencil anywhere on the bottom border of the map. Then draw a straight line. When you stop, don't lift the pencil. Complete your trip using one more straight line.

Answer on page 74.

Which Mountain?

Now that you've made it past the quicksand, it's time to do some climbing. You have a choice of climbing one of three geometrically shaped mountains, which are all 10,000 feet high. One of the mountains is a perfect cylinder, another is in the shape of a cone, and the third looks like the top half of a sphere. Several out-of-work math teachers have constructed roads that go from the base to the summit of each mountain. All three roads are built so that you climb 1 vertical foot every 20 horizontal feet. If you wish to walk the shortest distance from base to summit, which mountain would you choose?

Answer on page 75.

Compass Caper
✦ ✦ ✦

A compass is a reliable tool that always points north—or does it? There are many reports of compass needles that unexpectedly turn away from north. The strangest natural cause for this disturbance may be a shooting star. As the meteor streaks across the sky, it upsets the electrical balance of the air and produces a magnetic force that some believe effects the compass reading.

We, however, will work with a compass that always gives a true heading. Suppose you start a hike by traveling directly south for 500 paces. Then, you turn and go due east for another 100 paces. You turn once more and go due north for 500 paces. You are now in the exact same spot where you started from, but in front of you is a bear. What color is it?

Answer on page 75.

A Cut Above

With all that hiking, you've probably now worked up an appetite. So how about some pizza?

Suppose this is the early 1900s and you're in New York City's Little Italy getting a Pizza Margherita, named in honor of a pizza-loving Italian princess. Can you divide the pie into eight equal slices in only three straight cuts? All the pieces must be identical: each with an upper surface covered with sauce, lower baked crust, and a crusty edge.

HINT:
Don't worry
about the mess.
You won't have
to clean it.

Answer on page 75.

Kitchen Cups

✦ ✦ ✦

Have you ever seen the written form of the Sanskrit language? If so, you probably are amazed at how different this ancient language from India looks from ours. Some English words, however, are based on Sanskrit. For example, cup comes from the Sanskrit word *kupa*, which means water well. This puzzle requires several water wells.

Suppose you need to measure exactly 1 cup of water. All that you have in your kitchen are two containers. The smaller container holds 3 cups and the larger holds 5 cups. How can you use these two containers to measure exactly 1 cup of water?

Answer on page 75.

Moldy Math

✦ ✦ ✦

Now let's talk about something else that you might have, but not want, in your kitchen. While you are raiding the refrigerator, you look behind the stove and discover a slice of bread that you misplaced several weeks ago. Needless to say, it is covered with mold. Since the mold started growing, the area it has covered has doubled each day. By the end of the eighth day, the entire surface of the bread is covered. When was the bread half-covered with mold?

Answer on page 76.

And a Cut Below

✦ ✦ ✦

Have you ever heard of the cheesemobile? It's a giant refrigerated truck that was built to carry a piece of Cheddar cheese. Why, then, all the fuss? Simple. The cheese weighed over 40,000 pounds!

Take a look at the smaller barrel of cheese below. If you make these three complete and straight cuts, how many pieces of cheese will you have?

Answer on page 76.

Egg Exactly

✦ ✦ ✦

Suppose you have only two egg timers, a 5-minute and a 3-minute. Can you use these two measuring devices to time an egg that must be boiled for exactly 2 minutes?

WHY AGAIN DID YOU SAY YOU WANTED TO KNOW THIS?

Answer on page 76.

Losing Marbles?

✦ ✦ ✦

Marbles have been around for a long time. In fact, archaeologists have discovered marbles buried alongside an Egyptian child who died over 4000 years ago! The word "marble," however, comes from the Greek word *marmaros*, which is a white polished stone made from the mineral agate.

Now it's your turn to play with them. Place a marble in a cup and carry it to the opposite side of the room. Too easy, huh? To make this more challenging, the cup must be turned upside down. This may take a little bit of creative problem solving, but it can be done.

Answer on page 80.

A Puzzle of Portions

✦ ✦ ✦

Did you know that 3 ounces plus 3 ounces doesn't always equal 6 ounces? As illogical as this may sound, its true because of the behavior of the small particles (and spaces) that make up liquids. When different liquids are mixed, the particles tend to fill in some of the open spaces. As a result, the liquid becomes more compact and occupies less volume. It's only a small difference, but it is measurable.

Let's try mixing something whose volume does not change. Your challenge is to split some apple juice into three equal portions. The juice comes in a 24-ounce container. You have only three other containers, each holding 5, 11, and 13 ounces. How can you divide the juice into three equal portions?

HINT: At the very least, it will take four steps.

Answer on page 77.

Mixed Up?

✦ ✦ ✦

Root beer, not cola, is the oldest-marketed soft drink in America. Before it was sold in the United States, root beer was brewed in many colonial homes. It contained many ingredients including molasses, licorice, vanilla, and the bark from birch trees. It was going to be called root tea but was later changed to root beer to attract the tavern crowd.

Here is one 8-ounce cup filled with root beer and another 8-ounce cup filled with cola. Take 1 tablespoon of root beer and add it to the cola. Stir the mix-

OKAY, NOW STIR IT UP

ture. Now take 1 tablespoon of the mixture and add it to the root beer. Is there more root beer in the cola or cola in the root beer?

Answer on page 77.

Toothpick Teasers

✦ ✦ ✦

For the puzzles in this group, you can also use pieces of straws or small sticks if you don't have toothpicks.

These six toothpicks are arranged in a hexagon. Starting with this arrangement, can you form two identical diamonds by moving only two toothpicks and adding just one more?

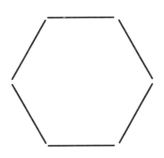

These sixteen toothpicks form eight identical triangles. Can you remove four toothpicks so that four of these triangles are left? All of the toothpicks that remain must be a side of the triangles with no loose ends sticking out.

Form four (and only four) identical squares by removing eight toothpicks.

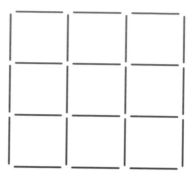

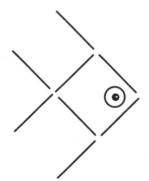

Move only three of the toothpicks (and the eye) to make the fish swim in the opposite direction.

Answers on pages 77–78.

Going to the Movies

✦ ✦ ✦

Let's take a break from these puzzles and go to the movies. The map below shows an assortment of routes from your home (H) to the movie theater (M).

If you can only to travel in a north, east, or northeast direction, how many possible routes are there from your home to the theater?

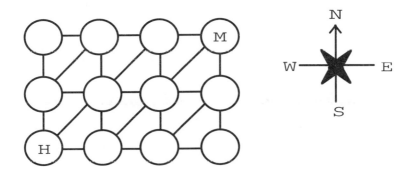

Answer on page 78.

Now Seating?

Suppose two boys and three girls go to the movie theater and they all sit in the same row. If the row has only five seats:

1. How many different ways can the two boys and three girls be seated in this row?
2. What are the chances that the two children at the ends of the row are both boys?
3. What are the chances that the two children at the ends of the row are both girls?

Answer on page 79.

Weighing In...

✦ ✦ ✦

The movie playing in the theater is about a scientist who changes into a fly. Before she transforms herself, she carefully weighs a jar of sleeping flies. Then, she shakes the jar to wake them up. While they are flying, the scientist weighs the jar again. Does the jar full of flies weigh less when the insects are flying?

Answer on page 79.

The Strangest Eyes

✦ ✦ ✦

The scientist has transformed herself into a fly. One of her eyes is made up of one loop coiled into a spiral-like design. The other eye is made up of two separate loops shaped into a similar design. Can you tell which eye is the single loop and which one is the double without tracing the lines with a pencil?

Answer on page 79.

Monkey Business

The theater shows a double feature. The second movie is about Tarzan going into the moving business.

For his first job, Tarzan must raise a 35-pound crate into his neighbor's tree house. To do this, he first attaches a pulley to a tree branch. He then passes a rope through the pulley and ties it to the crate. Just as he is about to lift the crate, he is called away to help a nearby elephant.

A passing chimp observes the situation and decides to help. The chimp also weighs 35 pounds. As the chimp pulls down on the rope what happens to the crate?

Answer on page 79.

Head Count

In the final scene, a pet store owner is counting the birds and lizards that Tarzan has delivered to her store. For some odd reason, she decides to tally only the heads and scaly legs of these animals. When she has finished, she has counted thirty heads and seventy legs. How many birds and how many lizards are there?

Answer on page 79.

Möbius Strip

✦ ✦ ✦

Here is one the strangest loops you'll ever see. It's called a Möbius strip in honor of the German mathematician who first investigated its properties.

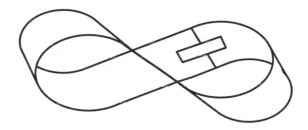

To build a Möbius strip, you need a strip of paper about 1 inch wide and 10 inches long. Coil the paper into a simple loop. Then put a single twist in the loop before securing the ends together with a piece of tape. Use a marker to color one side of the strip red and the other side blue. You'll soon discover that this loop has only one side!

Möbius strips are used in manufacturing. Many machines have belts that are used to connect different spinning parts. By using a belt sewn into a Möbius strip, the belt wears evenly on both sides.

Suppose you divide right down the middle of the Möbius strip. What shape would you get? Make a guess; then use a pair of scissors to carefully divide the strip.

Answer on page 80.

Aunt Möbius?

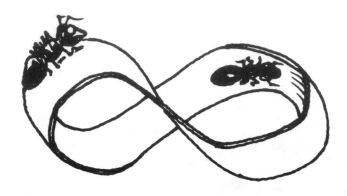

THINK ABOUT IT! If we place two ants side by side on a Möbius strip and start them off in opposite directions, they will first pass each other on opposite sides of the paper. Then one ant will be walking on the top side of the strip, while the other will be on the bottom side!

Ant Walk

Let's pick up an ant from the strip and place it on one corner of a sugar cube. This cube has sides all measuring 1 centimeter. If the ant can only walk along the edges of the cube, what is the total distance it can travel without retracing any part of its path?

Answer on page 80.

Cubic Quandaries

✦ ✦ ✦

A wooden cube is painted red. Suppose it is divided with six equal cuts into the smaller cubes as shown.

1. How many smaller cubes are there?
2. How many of these smaller cubes
   a. have only one side that is painted red?
   b. have two sides that are painted red?
   c. have three sides that are painted red?
   d. have no sides that are red?

Answers on page 80.

Squaring Off

✦ ✦ ✦

Make a copy of these four rectangles. Cut out the shapes and then arrange them to form a perfect square.

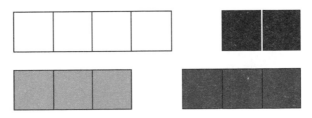

Answer on page 81.

Saving Face

✦ ✦ ✦

How good are you at visualizing things? These next few puzzles test your ability to rotate and construct objects in your mind.

These blocks below represent the same block. What figure is missing on the upper face of the last block?

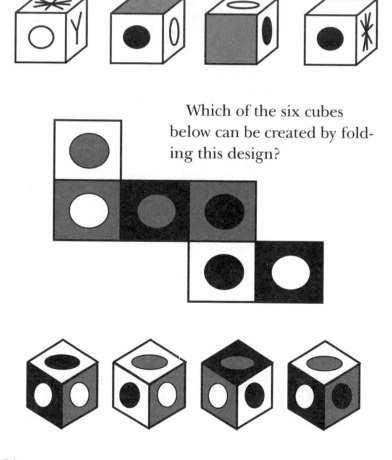

Which of the six cubes below can be created by folding this design?

Finally, if you fold up this flat sheet along the inner lines, which figure represents the result?

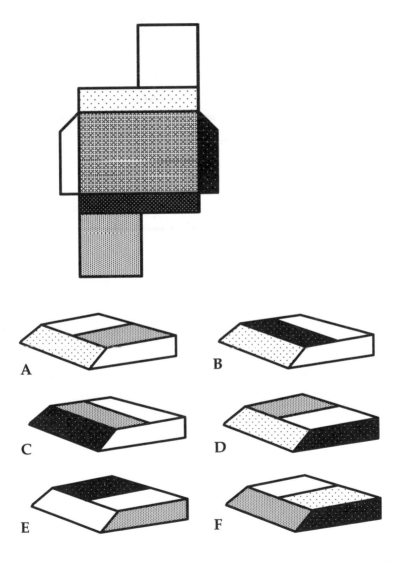

A

B

C

D

E

F

Answers on page 81.

Cut the Cards

✦ ✦ ✦

Have you ever played cards and wished you had a different hand? Suppose you need a heart instead of a spade. Well, here's your chance to change one suit into another.

Photocopy the spade below. Then use a pair of scissors to cut it into three pieces so that the pieces can be fitted together to form a heart. Can you do it?

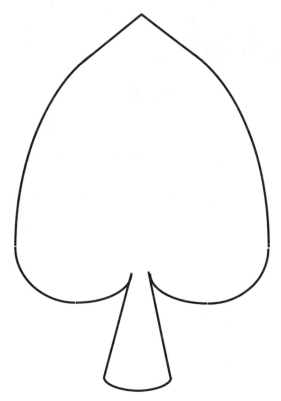

Answer on page 82.

Stripped Stripe

✦ ✦ ✦

There is a legend about a king who had six brothers and six sisters. His country's flag reflected this family structure with twelve bold stripes. When two of his brothers moved out of the kingdom, the king had two of the stripes removed.

Can you figure out how to cut the flag into as few pieces as possible so that the pieces can be put back together to make the same type of flag, but with two less stripes? No part of the flag can be discarded.

Answer on page 82.

Missing Square

✦ ✦ ✦

Count the number of blocks that make up this pattern. If you don't want to count each block, you can multiply the number of rows by the number of columns to get a total of sixty-four blocks.

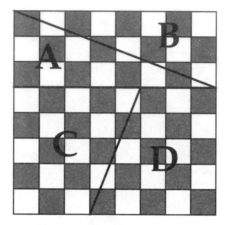

Now photocopy the pattern.

Using a pair of scissors, separate the checkerboard along the inner lines. Reassemble the pieces as shown below.

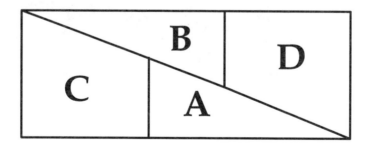

Now count the blocks, or, if you'd rather, just multiply again. The new figure is thirteen blocks long and five blocks high. That gives us sixty-five blocks. Where did the extra block come from?

Answer on page 83.

Tipping the Scales

✦ ✦ ✦

What whole animal(s) must be added to balance the fourth scale?

Answer on page 83.

Snake Spread

✦ ✦ ✦

These hungry snakes are swallowing each other. Since they began this odd dining experience, the circle they formed has gotten smaller. If they continue to swallow each other, what will eventually happen to the circle of snakes?

Answer on page 83.

Falcon Flight

✦ ✦ ✦

Two bicyclists are situated 60 miles apart. One has a falcon on his shoulder. The bicyclists start riding toward each other at the same time, both maintaining a constant speed of 30 mph. The moment they begin, the falcon flies off the first cyclist's shoulder and towards the other. The falcon flies at a constant ground speed of 45 mph. When the falcon meets the other rider, he reverses direction and flies back to the first cyclist (who is now considerably closer). The falcon continues this back and forth pattern until the riders finally meet. How far did the falcon fly?

Answer on page 83.

A Question of Balance

✦ ✦ ✦

Place two fingers at the ends of a yardstick. Slowly move the fingers toward each other. As you'll discover, your fingers always meet in the middle of the yardstick.

Now place both fingers in the middle of the stick. Slowly try moving the two of them out to the opposite ends. This time you'll find that one finger remains in the middle while the other moves to the end. Can you explain this behavior?

Answer on page 83.

Well-Balanced Plate

Here's a game that you are guaranteed to win as long as you let your opponent go first. Start with a plate on the exact center of a table. Your opponent must place another plate on the table. Then, it's your turn. During each turn, both of you must continue placing plates until no more plates will fit, but, don't worry, you'll win. Can you figure out the secret?

DOUBLE OR NOTHING ON YOUR ALLOWANCE? OKAY. BUT, YOU GO FIRST.

Answer on page 84.

Robot Walkers

Have you ever seen a robot walker? It is designed to move over various types of terrain so that scientists can use it to explore nearby planets. Our robot walkers are positioned at the corners of a square plot of land. Each robot is programmed to follow the robot directly ahead of it. If all the robots move at the same speed, what will happen to the square pattern? Will the robots ever meet?

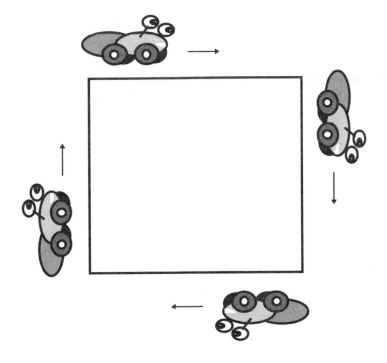

Answer on page 84.

Chain Links

✦ ✦ ✦

Suppose you own four pieces of chain. One chain has 5 links, two chains have 4 links, and one chain has 3 links.

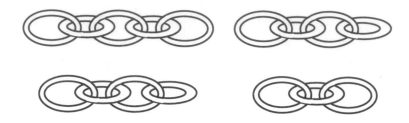

You go to the jeweler and ask her to make a bracelet using all of these chains. She says it would cost $.50 to break a link and $1.00 to weld a link together. You calculate that it would cost $6.00 to build the bracelet. The jeweler, however, says that it would only cost $4.50. Can figure out how she can assemble your bracelet for less?

Answer on page 85.

Rope Ruse

There is an old legend about an ancient magician who could tie a rope into a knot while holding on to each end of the rope. Can you?

Answer on page 85.

Money Magic

Look at the picture to your right. Can you guess what will happen when the bill is pulled from both ends?

After you've made your prediction, use a dollar bill and two paper clips to assemble this puzzle. Make sure that each paper clip grips only two of the three side-by-side sections. Slowly pull the bill apart. What happens to the clips? How is it possible?

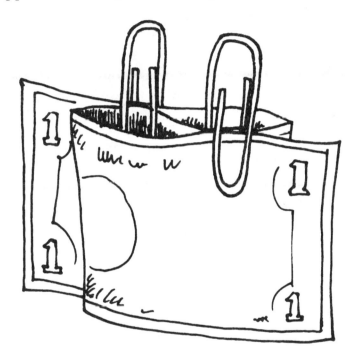

Answer on page 85.

Revolutionary Thoughts

✦ ✦ ✦

Different things orbit the earth at various speeds and distances. For example, satellites and space instruments released by the space shuttle are only several hundred miles away from the earth, while communication satellites circle at a distance of about 22,300 miles!

In this puzzle, Satellite X-1 orbits our planet once every 9 hours, Satellite Beta once every 4½ hours, and Satellite Parking once every 3 hours.

At time zero, the satellites are positioned in a straight line. How long will it take for all three objects to position themselves again in a straight line?

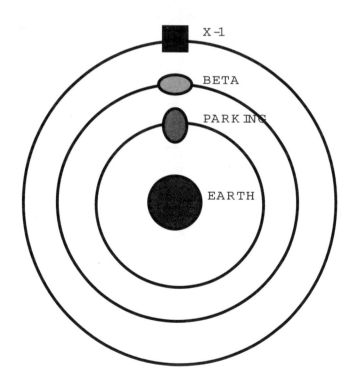

Answer on page 86.

Baffling Holes

✦ ✦ ✦

Black holes are celestial objects created by collapsed stars. These holes have tremendous concentration of matter and produce such a strong gravitational field that even light can't escape from it. If a black hole was placed on the surface of the earth, our entire planet would be sucked into it!

The hole in this puzzle is not as large as a black hole, but finding its solution can be a big challenge. Do you think a quarter can pass through a hole that is the size of a nickel? You can't tear, cut, or rip the hole. Impossible, you say? Trace the outline of a nickel onto an index card. Carefully cut out this outline.

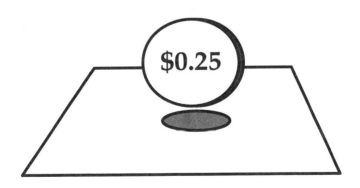

HINT: Bends and twists can open up a whole new geometry.

Solution on page 86.

A Giant Step

✦ ✦ ✦

Passing a quarter through a nickel-sized hole is nothing when you can step through an index card. Carefully use a pair of scissors or a modeling knife to cut out the pattern of slots shown here. When you are finished, the hole will open in an accordion-like style and allow you to step through it!

A Fair Solution

Two teenagers are deciding how to share the last piece of pizza. One of them must divide the slice. Both are afraid that the other will cut the slice unfairly and take the larger piece. Can this conflict be resolved by these teenagers so that both will be satisfied by the other one's cut?

After finishing their pizza, the happy teenagers bring out a box of toothpicks and arrange the toothpicks as follows:

Can you remove four toothpicks and leave ten on the table?

Answers on pages 86–87.

Sock It to Me

Did you know that a sock-like garment was first worn by Greek women? This soft leather covering appeared around 600 B.C. and was called a "sykhos." Roman women copied the style and changed the name to "soccus."

Let's open your "soccus" drawer. Suppose you have four pairs of black socks, three pairs of white socks, and a pair of red socks. It is nighttime and you can't see the colors of the socks. You need to select one pair of matching socks. Any color will do.

What is the least number of socks you need to remove from the draw to insure that you have at least one matching pair?

Answer on page 87.

Nuts!

✦ ✦ ✦

When you rotate a bolt clockwise, it travels into the threads of a nut. When that same bolt is rotated counterclockwise, the nut and bolt will separate.

Suppose you have two bolts aligned within each other's threads. If both bolts are rotated clockwise, will they move together, separate, or remain the same distance apart?

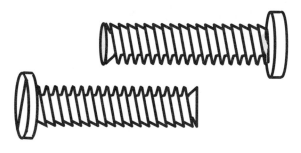

Here's something else to think about. In many large cities, the light bulbs used in places such as subway stations are unique. Instead of screwing into the socket with a clockwise motion, they require counter-clockwise turns. What sense does it make to have these different from most other bulbs?

Answers on page 87.

Doubtful Dimensions

John wants to ship a baseball bat to his sister. The bat is 4 feet, 11 inches long. He places it in a rectangular box that is 5 feet long. When he takes it to the shipper, they can't send the package because it is too long. All dimensions of the package must be 4 feet or less in order to be shipped.

When John returns home, he figures out how he can repack the bat. What does he do?

Answer on page 87.

Machine Madness

✦ ✦ ✦

The identical wheels of this machine are connected by a series of belts. The outer rim of each wheel has a circumference of 8 centimeters. The rim of each wheel's inner shaft has a circumference of 4 centimeters. If the crank is rotated up one-quarter turn, what hour would the clock's hand point to?

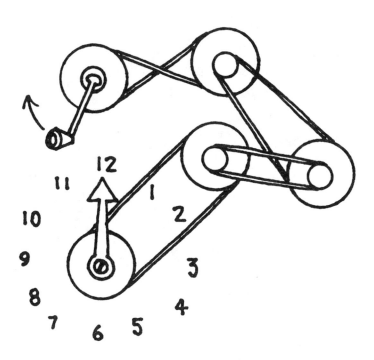

Answer on page 87.

Putting It Together

✦ ✦ ✦

Suppose you have a list of numbers from one to one hundred. How quickly can you add them all up without using a calculator?

HINT: There is a swift way to add these numbers. Think about how the numbers at the opposite ends of the list relate to each other.

Answer on page 88.

The Heat Is On

✦ ✦ ✦

The next time you drive under a highway bridge, take a close look at its ends. It is most likely that one end of the bridge will be attached directly to the road. The other end, however, will probably have a small gap. The gap is there on purpose. When the temperature rises, the bridge expands. If the gap wasn't there, the expanding metal bridge might shatter the roadway!

How about holes? Do they also expand when heated? Suppose a metal washer is placed in a flame. What happens to the size of its hole?

Answer on page 88.

City Pipes

✦ ✦ ✦

Beneath almost every city is an intricate system of large water-carrying pipes. These pipes transport runoff that falls through sewer openings and keep the city streets from flooding when there's a rainstorm.

The pipes are connected to the surface through manhole openings. Manhole covers fit over the openings. How does their shape prevent them from falling into the hole?

HINT: Think of how the bat from the "Doubtful Dimensions" puzzle on page 51 was packaged!

Answer on page 88.

Magic Square

Take a look at the grid below. Like the "Magic Pyramid" puzzle presented on page 9 of this book, the Magic Square is created when the right numbers are placed in the empty boxes.

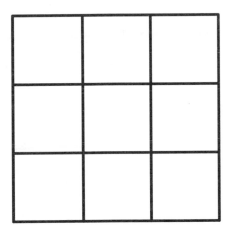

Place a number from 1 to 9 in each of the boxes below. Don't repeat any of the numbers. Their arrangement must result in any row of three numbers (vertical, horizontal, or diagonal) adding to 15.

Answer on page 89.

Anti-Magic Square

Like the Magic Square, the Anti-Magic Square uses the same grid as above, except you have to place the numbers 1 to 9 to create a square where each row's sum is *different*.

Think that's easy? Give it a try. Remember, you can't repeat any of the numbers.

Answer on page 89.

Numbers Game

Here's another game that you're bound to win as long as you let your opponent go first.

The object of the game is simple. The first one to reach 100 wins!

Each round involves adding a number from 1 to 10 to the previous number. Your opponent goes first and identifies a number from 1 to 10. You add to that number and announce the sum. The turns continue until 100 is reached.

The winning strategy is for you to always produce the key numbers, which are 12, 23, 34, 45, 56, 67, 78, 89, and the winning 100.

So if your opponent says 8, you add 4 and get to the first key number 12. You continue adding to the keys, and within nine rounds you'll be a winner.

Now suppose you can only add a number from 1 to 5 to your opponent's number until you reach 50.

What would the key numbers now be?

Answer on page 89.

What's Next?

✦ ✦ ✦

Take a look at the pattern below. These symbols have a logical order. Can you draw the next symbol in the sequence?

HINT: A little reflection with your thinking skills may help you solve this puzzle.

Answer on page 90.

Connect the Dots

✦ ✦ ✦

Starting at the top center dot, can you connect all of the other nine dots with only four straight lines? The four lines must all be connected and your pencil can't leave the paper while drawing the answer.

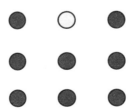

Answer on page 90.

Another Ant Walk

A queen ant finds herself climbing onto the metal framework of a bridge at the spot marked by the arrow.

Can you trace the path she'd need to follow in order to walk across every piece of frame only once and end up at the top of the bridge (marked by an X)?

Her path must be a continuous line.

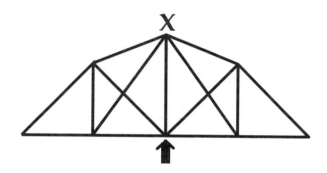

Answer on page 90.

In Order

✦ ✦ ✦

Examine the set of pictures on the next page. Can you place them in their most logical order?

Answer on page 91.

Tangrams

✦ ✦ ✦

In Asia, tangrams are known as "the seven plates of wisdom." No wonder, since this Chinese puzzle, probably one of the most famous dissection games, has been around for at least several hundred years.

A tangram consists of five triangles, a square, and a rhomboid.

To get these shapes, copy the lines shown below onto a square sheet of heavy stock paper. Use a pair of scissors to cut out each of the seven sections.

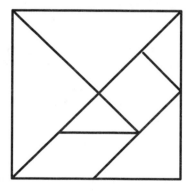

Another way you can make the seven shapes is to start with a square sheet of paper.
1. Cut the square in half to make two large triangles.

2. Cut one of the triangles in half to make two equal triangles (Sections I and II).

3. Fold back the corner of the other triangle and cut along this fold to get another triangle (Section III).

4. Cut the remaining piece into two equal halves.

5. Fold and cut one of the pieces to get a square and right triangle. (Sections IV and V).

6. Fold and cut the other piece like this (Sections VI and VII).

With your seven pieces, try and create these figures.

Answers on pages 91–92.

Fractured Farmland

While flying over farmland, a pilot notices the rectangular shape of the fields below. She sketches the lines that divide the fields.

When she returns to the airport, she wonders how many different rectangles can be formed by the lines drawn below?

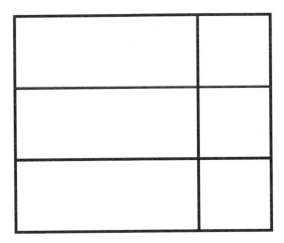

HINT: Don't forget that a square is also a rectangle.

Answer on page 92.

Number Sense

The number symbols we use are called Arabic numerals. Logically, they originated in the Middle East.

Right? Wrong. They were created in India. Europeans learned these symbols from Arabic scholars and, inadvertently, the name Arabic numeral stuck.

Now try not to get stuck on this number problem. Can you uncover the logic used to place each of the numbers below? If so, what number should be placed at the question mark?

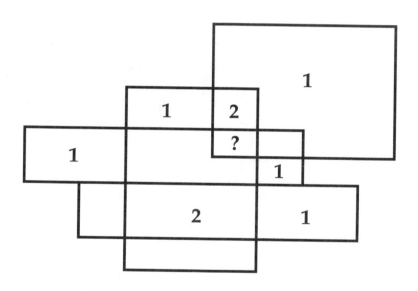

Answer on page 92.

What Comes Next?

✦ ✦ ✦

In the next page, choose the next logical member of the sequence.

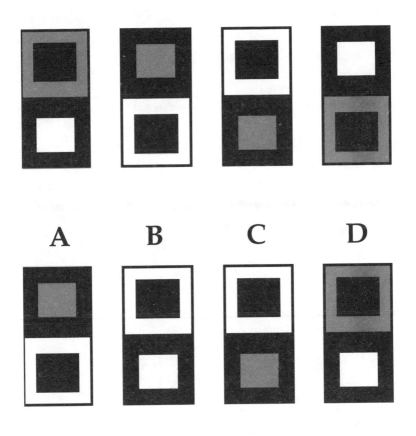

A   B   C   D

Answer on page 93.

The Marked Park

✦ ✦ ✦

Jethro's custom racer has two different-sized tires. The smaller front tire has a circumference of 7 feet. The larger rear tire has a circumference of 9 feet.

Rita, the meter maid, sees Jethro's racer parked in a 10-minute zone and decides to mark the curbside tires with a spot of paint. She places a mark on the front and rear tires exactly where each tire touches the ground.

Twenty minutes later, Rita returns. She sees both marks still touching the ground. As she begins writing a parking ticket, Jethro returns and explains that he did move his racer. In fact, he moved it the exact distance required to rotate the marks back into their same relative position. Assuming Jethro is telling the truth, what is the shortest distance that the racer was moved?

Answer on page 93.

Pattern Path

All of the numbers below form a sequence. Can you figure out the logic of the sequence? If so, begin at the point marked start and trace a path from box to box. The boxes can be connected horizontally, vertically, or diagonally. Double and triple digit numbers can be made by grouping the numbers this way. You can go through a box only once. Your mission is to finish at the stop sign located in the bottom right corner.

START

2	1	6	4	2	4
8	4	3	2	0	8
6	2	6	1	0	4
1	4	5	5	2	0
2	8	2	1	9	6

Answer on page 93.

Pile Puzzler

✦ ✦ ✦

Cards can be arranged in many different orders. Don't try all of them unless you have time to count 80,660,000,000,000,000,000,000,000,000,000,00 0,000,000,000,000,000,000,000,000,000,000

Here's a card challenge that has fewer solutions. Exchange one card from each of the piles to form three piles with equal sums.

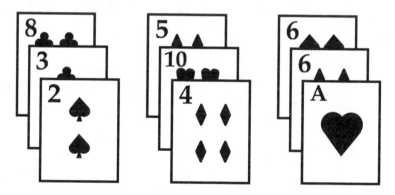

In this puzzle, the Ace only counts as one. Only one card can be exchanged from each pile.

Answer on page 93.

Pattern Puzzler

✦ ✦ ✦

The five numbers within each circle represent a mathematical relationship. This same relationship is displayed in each of the four circles.

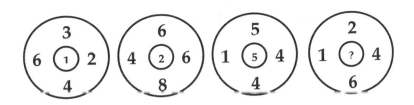

Using this pattern, what is the most likely value for the question mark in the last circle?

Answer on page 94.

Titillating Tiles

✦ ✦ ✦

There's a tile below that doesn't fit with the other four in the group.

Can you figure out the relationship of the tiles and find the one that is different?

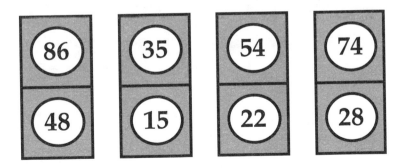

Answer on page 94.

Pattern Grid

A pattern grid is filled with items based on a geometric arrangement to form a visual pattern. Examine the grid below for a pattern and then try to select the section that completes it.

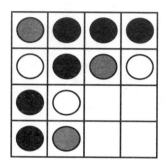

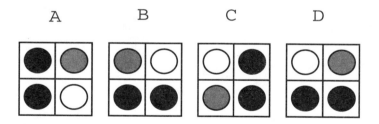

    A   B   C   D

Answer on page 94.

THE ANSWERS

Pyramid Passage

Magic Pyramid

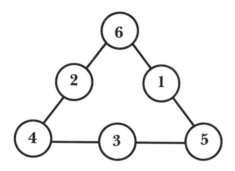

Pyramid Builders

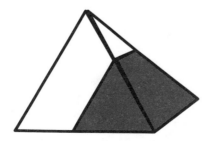

Trial by Triangle

1. In order to create these four equal triangles, you'll have to use all three dimensions. By constructing a three-dimensional pyramid shape, you'll create same-sized triangles on the structure's three sides and bottom.

2. Like the impossible triangle, these two objects are optical illusions and cannot be built.

Trapezoids 2 Triangle

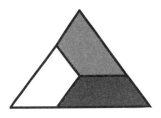

Spare My Brain

Since the four wheels of the three-wheel car share the journey equally, simply take three-fourths of the total distance (50,000 miles) and you'll get 37,500 miles for each tire.

Whirling Paradox

Relative to a stationary observer, the top of the wheel is moving faster than the bottom of the wheel. It all has to do with the forward motion of the car. Since the top half of the wheel is moving in the same direction as the car, their speeds are added together to obtain the relative speed of the moving upper spoke.

However, the lower spokes are moving in the opposite direction as the car. In this case, subtraction of the speeds results in a much slower relative speed—slow enough to count the individual spokes.

Lost?

To find out which way to go, you need to stand the sign back up.

Since you came from Skullara, align the sign so that the Skullara arrow points back to it. All the other arrows will then be pointed to the correct directions.

Sand Traps

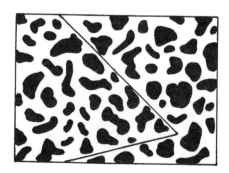

Which Mountain?

It doesn't matter which mountain you climb. All three paths will be the same length. The length of the path is not determined by the shape of the mountain but the slope of the road.

Since all three mountain paths have the same slope, you'd have to walk the same distance in order to climb each 10,000 foot summit.

Compass Caper

White. The bear must be a polar bear. To conform to the given pattern, the hiker must begin the trek at the magnetic North Pole.

A Cut Above

Make two cuts to divide the pizza along its diameter into four equal parts. Then stack the quarters on top of each other. Make another cut down the middle of the stack.

Although it might be messy, you'll have eight equal slices.

Kitchen Cups

Fill the three-cup container with water. Pour it into the five-cup container. Fill the three-cup container again, and fill up the five-cup container. This will leave you with exactly one cup of water in the three-cup container.

Moldly Math

This is simpler than it may seem. Since the mold doubles in size every day, it covered half as much area one day before!

And a Cut Below

Eight pieces as shown below:

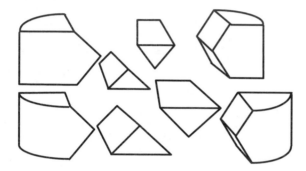

Egg Exactly

Simultaneously turn over the five and three minute timers when you begin to boil the water.

When the three minute timer runs out, put the egg into the boiling water. When the five minute timer runs out, the egg is done. Two minutes have elapsed.

Losing Marbles?

Start spinning the marble along the bottom of the cup so that it pushes against the inner wall.

When the spin is fast enough, the force overcomes the pull of gravity and the cup can be turned upside down.

A Puzzle of Portions

There are several ways to divide the juice. Here's one of the quickest:

Vessel size	24	13	11	5
To start	24	0	0	0
First	8	0	11	5
Second	8	13	3	0
Third	8	8	3	5
Fourth	8	8	8	0

Mixed Up?

There is the same amount of root beer in the cola as there is cola in the root beer.

For every drop of root beer that is in the cola cup, a drop of cola has been displaced and is in the root beer cup.

Toothpick Teasers

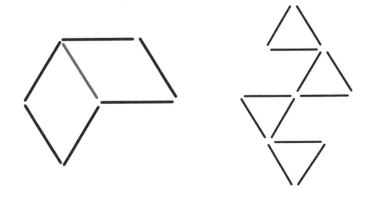

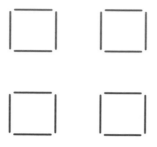

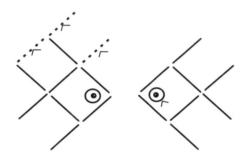

Going to the Movies

Tracing, counting, and remembering each step would drive you crazy. To make things easier, just write down the possible paths to each circle. The number of paths to the next circle is equal to the sum of the paths that connect to it.

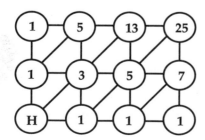

Now Seating?

1. There are ten possible combinations: BBGGG, BGBGG, BGGBG, BGGGB, GBBGG, GBGBG, GBGGB, GGBBG, GGBGB, GGGBB.

2. The chances for two boys being on the ends are 1 in 10.

3. The chances for two girls being on the ends are 3 in 10.

Weighing In...

The weight of the jar doesn't change. In order to fly, the insects must produce downward air currents that are equal in force to their weight. Therefore, whether standing or in flight, the insects push down with the same force.

The Strangest Eyes

Unfortunately, you will need to check this one by tracing over the pattern. As you do, you'll discover a single loop on the left and a double loop on the right.

Monkey Business

Both the crate and the chimp go up.

Head Count

Although this type of problem is perfect for algebra, let's do it visually. If all of the thirty heads belonged to two-legged birds, then there'd be only sixty legs. If one of the animals has four legs, then there'd be sixty-two legs. If two animals are four-legged, there'd be sixty-four legs.

By continuing in this pattern until we reach seventy legs, we will get a combination of twenty-five birds and five lizards.

Möbius Strip

The shape you get from dividing the Möbius strip is one large continuous loop with four twists.

Ant Walk

Nine centimeters. One basic pattern is illustrated below.

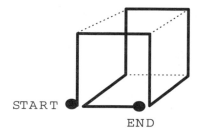

START
END

Although there are other turns, they cover the same total length.

Cubic Quandaries

There is a total of 27 cubes. There are six cubes with one red side, twelve cubes with two red sides, eight cubes with three red sides, and one cube with no red sides.

Squaring Off

Saving Face

1. The face should have a circle design.

2. The pattern folds into a cube that looks like this:

3. Folding the creases would produce this final version:

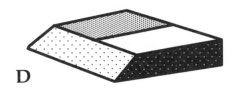

D

Cut the Cards

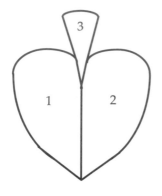 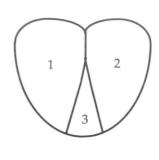

Stripped Stripe

Here is the cut pattern....

and here is the reassembly.

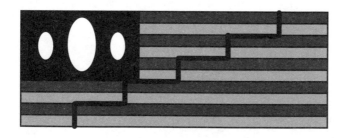

Missing Square

There isn't an extra block. The area making the new block was "shaved off" from some of the other blocks. The loss of each block's area is so small that it's not easy to observe.

Tipping the Scales

Snake Spread

The snakes will fill their stomachs and not be able to swallow anymore. The circle will then stop getting smaller.

Falcon Flight

The falcon's total distance is determined by the amount of time he was aloft and the speed he maintained.

The speed is given. The time is derived from the two cyclists. Since the cyclists are 60 miles apart and drive towards each other at 30 mph, the total time elapsed is 2 hours. The bird flying at 45 miles per hour will cover 90 miles in this 2-hour period.

A Question of Balance

It has to do with friction, balance, and the weight of the yardstick.

As you move your fingers towards the middle of the yardstick, the balance of the yardstick shifts. The finger that is closer to the middle will support more weight, making it easier for the other, more distant finger to "catch up" and move closer to the middle as well. This "catching up" flip-flops between the two fingers until they both arrive at the middle of the yardstick.

The finger that moves first from the middle immediately bears less of the ruler's weight, which makes it easier for this finger to keep moving. The farther it moves, the easier sliding becomes.

Well-Balanced Plate

You must mirror your opponent's placement of the plate. This way, as long as he has a place for his plate, you have a place for yours.

Robot Walkers

The robots follow a path that forms a continually shrinking and rotating square. Eventually, the robots will meet in the middle of the square.

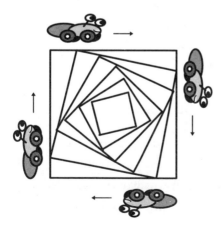

Chain Links

Select the chain with three links. Break open one of the links and use it to connect any two of the other sections. Break another of its links and use it to connect two other sections. Break the third and final link and use it to make a complete loop.

Rope Ruse

Fold your arms as shown above. Then, pick up the free end of the rope while your arms are already crossed. As you uncross your arms, the rope will automatically knot itself.

Money Magic

The clips will lock together and drop off the bill. A paper clip isn't a complete loop. It has two stretched openings through which the clip can slip off the bill. As the two sections of the bill move by each other, the clips slip through their openings and are pushed together to "reclip" onto each other's loop.

Revolutionary Thoughts

Four and a half hours. In order to be in a straight line the satellites must travel either one full revolution or one-half revolution. In 4½ hours, they'll look like this:

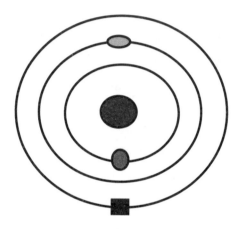

Baffling Holes

Fold the card in half so that the circular hole is also folded in half. Then slightly twist the paper as you pass the quarter snugly through the hole.

A Fair Solution

1. Either teenager can cut the slice, but the other person selects who gets which slice.

2. The four removed toothpicks leave the word "TEN."

Sock It to Me

Four socks. In a worst case scenario, if you draw three socks, each of a different color, the next sock you draw guarantees a matching color.

Nuts!

1. As you rotate each screw in a clockwise direction, they come together.
2. City-owned bulbs have opposite threads so that they won't screw into the standard light sockets that people have in their homes. Therefore, this discourages theft.

Doubtful Dimensions

A box with 3 × 4 dimensions has a diagonal length of 5 feet.

Machine Madness

Midway between 10 and 11 o'clock. The rotation decreases from one-quarter turn to one-eighth turn between the second and third wheel.

As the smaller hub of the second wheel rotates one-quarter turn, it moves the attached belt by only 1 foot. The 1-foot belt movement spins the larger third wheel only one-eighth of a revolution. This one-eighth turn remains the same for the fourth and fifth wheel. The belt twist between the first and second wheel changes the spin from clockwise to counterclockwise.

Putting It Together

The list contains fifty pairs of numbers that add to 100 (100+0, 99+1, 98+2, 97+3, etc.) with the number 50 as an unpaired leftover. $50 \times 100 + 50 = 5,050$.

The Heat Is On

As the washer expands, so does the hole it forms. Think of the washer as an image being stretched on a graphics program. Both the washer and its encircled hole will enlarge.

City Pipes

It is impossible for the round sewer cover to fall into the round pipe.

If the cover and tube had rectangular dimensions, the cover would be able to slip into the tube by being tilted in diagonally. But no matter how you tilt the circular cover, it can't fit through a hole of the same dimension.

Magic Square

8	3	4
1	5	9
6	7	2

Anti-Magic Square

5	1	3
4	2	6
8	7	9

Numbers Game

The trick to figuring out the key numbers is to keep subtracting the maximum you can add plus one beginning with the starting number.

For instance, because you can only use the numbers 1–5, if you work in increments 6 down from 50, you will get your key numbers: 8, 14, 20, 26, 32, 38, 44.

What's Next?

The symbols are the mirror images of the numbers 1 to 4 rotated on their side. The next image is a 5, modified in the same way.

Connect the Dots

The trick to this challenge is that the line can go out of the grid. Otherwise, it is impossible to complete.

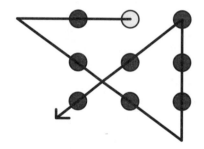

Another Ant Walk

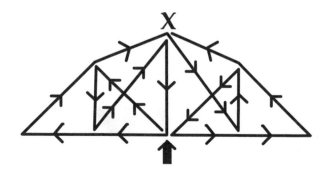

In Order

1. Girl walks to right wearing raingear and umbrella, passes grocery store, in the heavy rain.
2. Girl walks to right, passes record store, wearing raingear and umbrella, in less rain.
3. Girl stops, umbrella up, she holds out hand to feel rain. There is no rain.
4. Girl has stopped, folds up umbrella. There is no rain.
5. Girl walks to left, holds folded umbrella, passes record store. There is no rain.
6. Girl walks to left, holds folded umbrella, passes grocery store. There is no rain.
7. Girl walks to right holding baseball bat, passes grocery store. It is sunny.
8. Girl walks to right, passes record store, holds baseball bat. It is sunny.

Tangrams

Fractured Farmland

Eighteen: one whole composite block (1,2,3,4,5,6); six separate blocks (1) (2) (3) (4) (5) (6); three horizontal pairs (1&4) (2&5) (3&6); four vertical pairs (1&2) (2&3) (4&5) (5&6); two vertical triplets (1,2,3) (4,5,6); two large blocks (1,4,2&5) (2,5,3&6)

1	4
2	5
3	6

Number Sense

Three. Each number identifies the numbers of overlapping rectangles that cover that space.

What Comes Next?

D. During each step, the colors advance from outside top to inside top to inside bottom to outside bottom to outside top.

The Marked Park

Sixty-three feet. The lowest common multiple between the small wheel (7 feet) and large wheel (9 feet) is obtained by multiplying seven and nine.

Pattern Path

The sequence of the path is made by multiplying the digits by two: 2,4,8,16,32,64,128, etc. Here's a small part of that path:

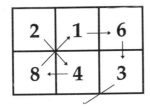

Pile Puzzler

To make things easy, first find the total value for each pile by adding up all the card values. Divide the sum (forty-five) by three to get the value for each pile (fifteen).

10	6	6
2	5	A
3	4	8

Pattern Puzzler

Three. The central number (E) is obtained by dividing the product of the top (A) and bottom (B) numbers by the product of the right (D) and left (C) numbers. $A \times B/C \times D = E$.

 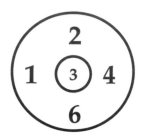

Titillating Tiles

54/22. With the other tiles, when you multiply the individual digits of the top number, you arrive at the bottom number. For example: $4 \times 8 = 32$.

Pattern Grid

D. The grid is divided into four 4×4 tiles. As you go in a "Z" pattern from the top left tile to right to bottom left to right, you'll see that the tile rotates one-quarter turn.

INDEX

Page key: puzzle, *answer.*

About the Author

Michael DiSpezio has always had a fondness for integrating learning with creativity, critical thinking, and performance. After tiring of "counting hairs on copepods," Michael traded the marine science laboratory for the classroom. Over the years, he has taught physics, chemistry, mathematics, and rock 'n' roll musical theater. During his classroom years, Michael co-authored a chemistry book, which launched his writing career.

To date, Michael is an author of eighteen science textbooks, a producer of several educational videos, and a creator of hundreds of supplementary products and science education articles. Michael's expertise in both video and science education resulted in several trips to train counterparts in the Middle East. When he isn't presenting workshops for science teachers, Michael's at home writing, creating, and puzzle solving.